PLAY
BETTER GOLF
WITH
JOHN JACOBS

PLAY
BETTER GOLF
WITH
JOHN JACOBS

Written in collaboration with Ken Bowden

Stanley Paul
London   Sydney   Auckland   Johannesburg

Stanley Paul & Co. Ltd

An imprint of Century Hutchinson Ltd

62–65 Chandos Place, London WC2N 4NW

Century Hutchinson Australia (Pty) Ltd
PO Box 496, 16–22 Church Street,
Hawthorne, Melbourne, Victoria 3122

Century Hutchinson New Zealand Limited
PO Box 40-086, Glenfield, Auckland 10

Century Hutchinson South Africa (Pty) Ltd
PO Box 337, Bergvlei 2012, South Africa

First published January 1969
Reprinted 1969 (three times), 1971, 1972, 1973,
1975, 1978, 1980, 1982, 1983, 1985, 1986, 1989 (redesigned)

© Yorkshire Television 1969

Set in Linotron Plantin/Helvetica

Printed in Great Britain by Mackay's, Letchworth

ISBN 0 09 0969103

CONTENTS

Acknowledgements

The author and publishers would like to thank David Cannon of AllSport, who took all the photographs in this book.

Our thanks, too, to the New Forest Golf Club for letting us use their facilities.

John Jacobs – Golf Doctor

John Jacobs is a physically active instructor. Standing behind the pupil and looking down the line (i.e. keeping him or her between himself and the target-line), he can readily see the flight path of the ball and what the clubhead is doing to produce it. From that vantage point, the two planes of the swing – the turn of the shoulders and the movement of the arms and club – are seen in clear perspective. 'Remember,' he will say, 'the shoulders go back and the arms go up.'

One might think that, with such a process, he would be glad to resort to a shooting stick or seat. But that wouldn't suit him. He is constantly moving about, watching the flight of the shot and then moving forward to help a pupil make an adjustment, tee up another ball or provide one of those simple and easily understood demonstrations. He is never still.

But it's not just as the practical analyst, extolling the virtues of ball flight, impact and ball control, that John Jacobs offers guidance. He has always been one for encouraging the art, particularly among the young, of getting the golf ball round the course – 'getting it up and down'.

P.B. 'LADDIE' LUCAS
(former Walker Cup captain)

1
Fundamentals
The three golfing dimensions

When you swing a golf club, what basically are you trying to do? What is the fundamental objective of all the movements you make?

Probably every golfer would supply a different answer, so we shall save time if I tell you the right one. The fundamental objective of all the movements you make when you have a golf club in your hands, on every shot from the drive to the putt, is to get the clubhead to meet the ball correctly. You may use a variety of devices to help you do that – pivot, weight transference, head still, wrist-cock, etc. – but these are not objectives in themselves. In the final analysis, proper impact of club on ball is what produces good golf shots.

Which leads us to another question: what is proper impact?

Here, in the simplest possible terms, is the answer. Your clubhead will contact the ball correctly when, at the moment of impact:

1. It's face is square – at right angles – to your target-line

2. The direction, or line, of your swing coincides with your target-line.
3. The angle of the club's approach is such that it allows the face or blade to hit solidly into the back of the ball.

If you always meet those three objectives, you will always hit the ball straight and solidly, whatever sort of swing you possess – the laws of mechanics won't let you do anything else. If you get one or more of them wrong, however elegant or orthodox a swinger you may appear to be, your shots will be misdirected and mishit.

It is because they never properly understand these vital golfing dimensions – as I like to call them – that the game is such a struggle for many people. They spend years practising and playing, reading books, taking lessons, and fiddling about with their swings, without ever getting to the real roots of the problem. Curing faults depends on correct diagnosis, and correct diagnosis depends on understanding the game's mechanical cause and effect. If you can't or won't do that, your approach to golf must always be that of a man playing blind man's buff: hit and hope.

So I am afraid I shall not, like most teachers, take you straight into physical swing technique. I want you first to exercise your mind. I want to take you into golfing cause and effect: show you exactly how the three dimensions set out above control the flight of the ball. And we'll do it the proper way, by fully analysing the four flight patterns a golf ball can follow, other than straight. So here goes with the thinking caps.

Slice A slice is a shot that starts to the left of target, then curves to the right. It is the standard shot of 95 per cent of the world's golfers, and the weakest shot in the game. Its mechanical causes are as follows:

1. The clubface is open, or pointing right of target, at impact.

2. The direction of the swing, or swing-line, is across the target-line from the farside to the nearside of the ball – from out-to-in.

3. The angle of the club's approach to the ball is steeply downward.

These three errors interact, at impact, as follows:

The ball is started to the left of target because the swing-line is in that direction. But the clubface is open to that line, which means that it is dragged across the ball with a pronounced cutting action. This imparts left-to-right sidespin to the ball. At the same time the steeply downward angle of the club's approach prevents the clubface from making solid contact with the back of the ball – it can only strike the upper half a glancing blow. The combined effect of all these factors is to minimise forward thrust, and allow the

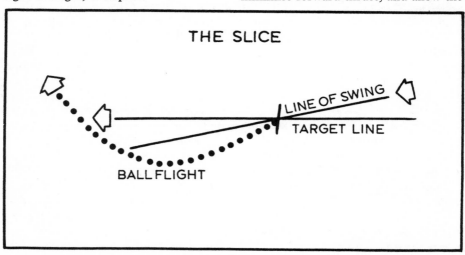

THE SLICE

LINE OF SWING

TARGET LINE

BALL FLIGHT

12

sidespin quickly to take over, bending the ball to the right.

It is obvious, therefore, that a golfer who slices has somehow got to cure three mechanical faults: He has to square-up his clubface, bring his swing-line around to the right so that it coincides with his target-line, and flatten out his angle of approach so that the club travels more parallel to the ground in the hitting area, and thereby meets the back rather than the offside top of the ball.

Pull A pull is a shot that flies straight all the way, but left of target. Many golfers, who don't understand the basic mechanics of golf, confuse it with a hook, in which the ball also finishes left of target. But hookers rarely pull. The shot derives from the type of swing that produces sliced shots, as we'll see when we look at its mechanical causes:

1. The direction of the swing, or swing-line, is across the target-line from out-to-in.
2. The clubface is *square* to the swing-line (facing in the same direction), but *closed* to the target-line (facing to the left of it).

They interact at impact as follows:

The ball is started to the left of target because the swing-line is in that direction, exactly the same as in a slice. But, because the clubface is square to the *swing-line* – facing in the same direction – no sidespin is imparted. Hence the ball continues to fly straight in the direction of the swing-line.

The golfer who pulls, therefore, has to cure only one mechanical fault: his swing direction. When he does that, his clubface at impact will automatically square up with his target-line, and the ball will fly straight to the target.

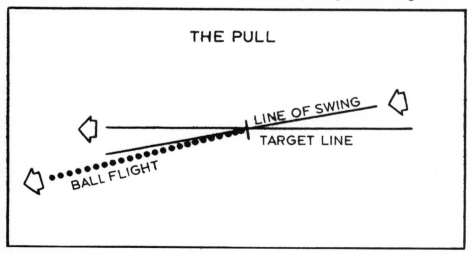

THE PULL

LINE OF SWING

TARGET LINE

BALL FLIGHT

Hook A hook is the opposite of a slice, a shot starting right of target then curving to the left. It is the bugbear of the good or strong player, and the mechanical factors behind it at impact are as follows:

1. The clubface is closed, or pointing left of target.

2. The direction of the swing, or swing-line, is across the target-line from the nearside to the farside, or in-to-out.

3. The angle of the club's approach to the ball is shallow – close to the ground well before impact.

These factors interact in exactly the opposite way to a slice, as follows:

The ball is started to the right of target, because the swing-line is in that direction. But the clubface is closed, which generates right-to-left sidespin and drives the ball in flight from right-to-left. The shallow angle of the club's approach forces the golfer either to catch the ground behind the ball or half-top the shot. This type of swing produces a lot of forward thrust, but the strong sidespin bends the ball to the left in the latter part of its flight, and it is difficult to make a good impact unless the ball is teed-up.

From this, it is apparent that a golfer who hooks has to work, like the slicer, on all three mechanical faults: he has to square-up the clubface, bring his swing-line around to the left so that it coincides with his target-line, and steepen his angle of approach so that the clubhead travels more sharply downward in the hitting area, and thereby meets the back rather than the inside bottom of the ball.

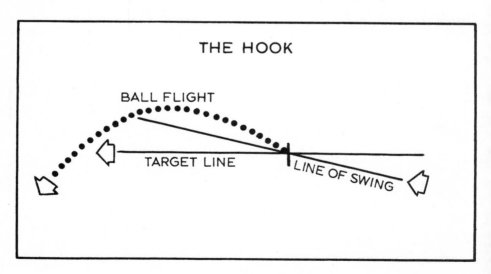

THE HOOK

BALL FLIGHT

TARGET LINE

LINE OF SWING

Push A push is a shot that travels straight all the way but right of target. Many golfers confuse it with a slice, because of where the ball finishes. In fact, it derives from the sort of swing that hooks, and here's why mechanically:

1. The direction of the swing, or swing-line, is across the target-line from in-to-out, as with a hook.
2. The clubface is *square* to the swing-line (facing in the same direction), but *open* to the target-line (facing to the right of it).

The interaction at impact here is the exact opposite of a pull. The ball is started right of target because the swing-line is in that direction, but, because the clubface matches the swing-line, no sidespin is imparted and it continues to fly straight.

Consequently, the golfer who pushes, like the golfer who pulls, has to cure only one mechanical fault: his direction of swing. When he brings that round so that it coincides with his target-line, his clubface automatically squares up and the ball flies straight to the target.

Now, I appreciate that the game viewed in these terms will be foreign to many golfers, but I would ask them to study and re-study this opening chapter until the three dimensions I have explained, and their interaction upon each other, become crystal clear. For it is only when he can tell from the behaviour of the ball what his clubhead is doing at impact that a golfer comes within easy reach of fulfilling his physical potential at the game. Any other way involves ceaseless experiment and, through that, endless frustration.

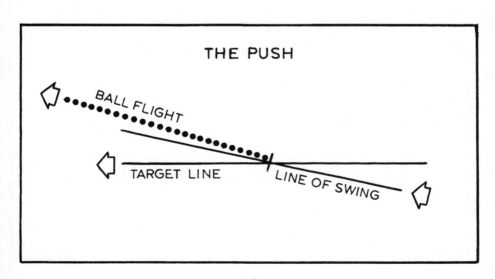

THE PUSH

BALL FLIGHT

TARGET LINE

LINE OF SWING

Above all, I would ask you to remember right through this book, and at all times when you are working on your game, the three factors that produce a straight shot. They are: the clubface square to the target-line, the direction of the swing coinciding with the target-line, and an angle of approach that allows the clubhead to hit solidly into the back of the ball.

Let's now relate them to the swing itself.

How the three basic dimensions of golf – clubface alignment, direction of swing and angle of approach – determine the flight of the ball

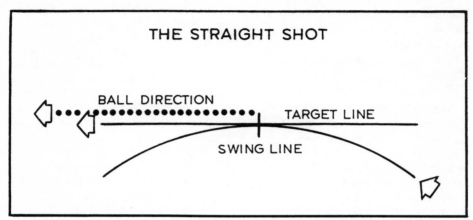

THE STRAIGHT SHOT

BALL DIRECTION

TARGET LINE

SWING LINE

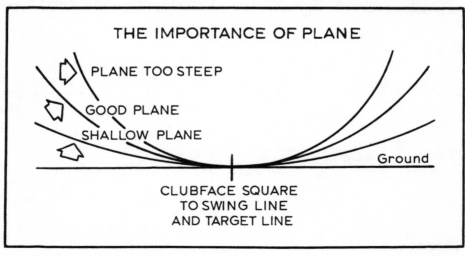

THE IMPORTANCE OF PLANE

PLANE TOO STEEP

GOOD PLANE

SHALLOW PLANE

Ground

CLUBFACE SQUARE
TO SWING LINE
AND TARGET LINE

2

Set-up

The vital starting points

Our focus in considering the golfing dimensions was upon impact – the proper arrival of the club at the ball. Now, knowing exactly what we are trying to do at that critical point, we can move back to the start, and consider how best we can set-up the golf club and ourselves to meet those objectives.

Which way the clubface will be pointing at impact is controlled primarily by your grip, the way you hold the club. So is another important golfing factor we haven't yet considered – clubhead speed. You need a grip that will not simply swing the clubface through the ball squarely aligned to your target, but one that will do so *fast* – because distance in golf is entirely the result of clubhead speed correctly applied.

What is such a grip? I am afraid that you are the only person who can answer that question, by carefully experimenting in the way you hold the club until you discover exactly the formula that gets the job done for *you*, a unique individual. The best I – or any other teacher – can do is to show you the grip principles that, over many years, have been found to make returning the clubface square to the ball at speed easiest for the greatest number of golfers.

Start by placing the club diagonally across your open left hand, so that it lies in the crook of the first finger and across the palm under the butt of the thumb, with about half an inch of shaft protruding. Then close your left hand over the shaft, with the thumb riding just to the right side of the shaft. If you are correct so far, you will find that your last three fingers are pressing the club firmly against your palm; that the 'V' formed by the thumb and forefinger is pointing between your chin and right shoulder when you ground the club with the face square to your target; and that, when you look down, you can see between two and three knuckles of your left hand.

Now add your right hand to your left, by bringing it onto the shaft as close as is comfortably possible below the left hand, in such a way that, if you

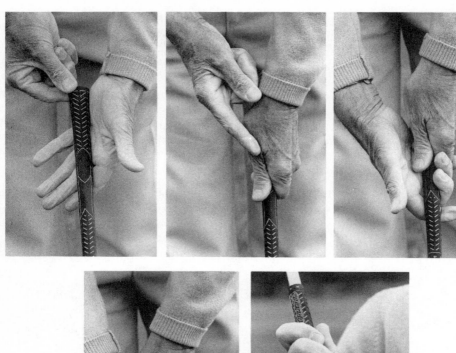

Building a sound grip. The left hand goes on to the club first, and is followed by the right hand to make a snug, balanced unit. The grip controls the alignment of the clubface at impact

opened both hands, your palms would be directly opposed. Do this correctly and you will find that the shaft nestles neatly across the roots of the fingers of your right hand, and that you are gripping chiefly with the second and third fingers. Check next that the right thumb is slightly to the left side of the shaft; that the left thumb rests snugly in the palm of your right hand; and that your right forefinger is slightly 'triggered' around the shaft.

If it helps to make your hands feel like a single unit, wrap the little finger of your right hand around the forefinger of the left (the orthodox overlapping grip), or lock it between the forefinger and second finger of the left hand (the interlocking grip). If you have very small or weak hands, do neither, but simply be sure that your hands fit snugly together. Finally, check that the 'V' formed by the thumb and forefinger of the right hand points to the same spot between your chin and right shoulder as the left-hand 'V'.

Remember that the flight of the ball will always tell you whether your grip is returning the clubface square to the target. If your shots bend in the air, it is not. If you are consistently slicing, your grip is leaving the clubface open at impact, and you may need to strengthen it by moving both hands as a unit – a bit at a time – to the right. If you are hooking regularly, your grip is closing the club face at impact, and you may need to weaken it by moving both hands – again as a unit – to the left.

Only by intelligent experiment can a golfer establish his own perfect grip; there is no one formula applicable to everyone, whatever you may previously have read or been told about golf.

As the grip takes care of the clubface, so the way you aim and stand to the ball at address will largely determine the direction of your swing – the second vital golfing dimension.

We have seen that, if the ball is to be started straight, the swing-line and the target-line must coincide at impact – in other words, the clubhead must not be coming to the ball from the outside or the inside, but straight along the target-line. By far the easiest way of ensuring that this happens is to align yourself perfectly parallel to the target-line when you address the ball. If you do not, the direction of your swing at impact will naturally follow your address alignment: it will be across the ball from out-to-in if you are aimed left of target, or across in the other direction – from in-to-out – if you are aimed right of target.

It is because they do not appreciate the importance of correct aim and alignment that a lot of golfers never score as well as they swing. They can generate motive force all right, but they don't direct it accurately at the outset, so, if the ball goes where they intend it to, it is really just a lucky accident.

The most common error of all in getting ready to play a golf shot, of which 99 per cent of club players are guilty, is plonking the feet down, *then* placing the club behind the ball. Correct clubface aim and body alignment can only be a sheer fluke if you tackle things in this order. Another major error – which even good golfers make – is to assume that, because the feet are placed parallel to the target-line, the rest of the body automatically assumes that alignment.

There is a positive procedure for setting-up to hit a golf ball straight to a target, which I want you to study, practise and build firmly into your game. It is as follows:

1. Take the club in your hands as you approach the ball from behind, i.e., looking down the target-line and forming a mental picture of the shot.

2. Take your grip – the grip that will return the clubface square and at speed for *you* – as you move round to the side of the ball.

3. With your grip formed, place the clubhead behind the ball so that the *bottom* edge of the face is exactly at right angles to your target-line. *Always* do this, with every club in the bag, before you take your stance.

4. Now move into position, so that you yourself are at right angles to the

The set-up, with the grip the most important factor in golf. You aim the clubface squarely at the target, and then you stand to the clubface. This places you parallel to the target-line, especially with your shoulders

Since the left hand is above the right, the left shoulder is higher than the right

clubface – or, to put it another way, parallel to your target-line.

5. Check – and re-check – that, whatever alignment your feet take (and to some extent you can let comfort dictate that), your *shoulders and upper body* are parallel to your target-line. Never forget that it is this area of you that establishes and controls the direction of your swing. If you aim your shoulders left at address, your swing will tend to be out-to-in at impact, and if you aim them right, it will be in-to-out. Whatever else you forget about golf, never forget this.

A very good gimmick for setting-up in this way is to imagine that the ball is on one railway line and that you are standing on the other. The far rail is your target-line. You are correctly set-up for your swing-line to coincide with your target-line when every part of you – feet, knees, hips, chest, shoulders – aligns exactly with the rail on which you are standing.

I might add that if you follow this procedure correctly, ball position relative to your feet will take care of itself. If the clubface is square, and you are square to the clubface, the ball will

(Left) All set up for a slice. The shoulders are aimed left of the target and the natural swing-line will be in the same direction, bringing the club steeply across the ball from out-to-in. *(Right)* the hooker's set-up. Shoulders are aimed right of the target, which throws the swing-line from in-to-out and creates a flat angle of attack

automatically be correctly located for the club you are using.

We have seen that alignment of the clubface is controlled by the grip, and the direction of the swing by how a golfer aims.

Finally, in relating the set-up to the three vital dimensions of golf, we come to the angle of the club's approach to the ball.

What controls the angle of clubhead approach is the plane of your swing, and this in turn is largely dependent on your posture and stance at address.

If you bend over the ball with your legs straight and your head and hands low, the only way it is physically possible to swing the club straight back from the ball is in a steep or upright plane – along a path much nearer to vertical than horizontal. Obviously, unless some correction is made during the swing – an inside looping movement – the club will return to the ball along an equally steep approach path, and you will have difficulty in getting the face squarely into the back of the ball; you will be giving it a downward rather than a forward blow.

On the other hand, if you stand very erect from your hips to your shoulders, with your knees exaggeratedly bent and your head and hands high, your natural swing plane will be shallow or flat – along a path much nearer to horizontal than vertical. Again, unless a mid-swing compensation is made, the club will return along a correspondingly flat approach path and you will be hard put to contact the ball before the club touches the ground; you will be coming in too shallow.

So, at address, you obviously need to establish a happy medium between a very upright and a very flat swing plane, and the way to do that is to relate your posture to your build and height.

If you are tall, you will need to stand tall, with your knees well flexed and your head and hands high, to prevent your swing assuming too steep a path. In this case, you will stand fairly close to the ball, with just enough room between your arms and body to make a full swing. Conversely, if you are short, you will need to lean over from the waist with your legs straighter, so that the club does not follow too shallow a path. In this case, you will stand farther away from the ball with more 'daylight' between your arms and body.

In either case you must be prepared to experiment a little to establish for yourself the angle or plane of swing that brings the club solidly into the back of the ball, not the top half of it nor the ground behind it.

We have now dealt with the set-up in relation to the three golfing dimensions. Before we move on to the swing – remember, we haven't so much as moved the club back from the ball yet – I want to let you into a secret.

Opposite: Address posture establishes the plane of the swing – the steepness or shallowness of the club's approach to the ball. This golfer is being persuaded to stand 'taller' to alter the plane of a swing that was too steep

22

If you can get your grip, your aim and your stance right, you are 85 per cent of the way to becoming a good golfer. And I'm not kidding. Every top player will confirm that these 'statics' – the pre-swing preparations – are the make-or-break factors in golf.

Get them wrong, and you make a really good swing virtually impossible. Get them right, and you give yourself a 100 per cent chance of hitting good shots with a minimum amount of experiment, adjustment or compensation.

3
The Backswing
What is a backswing for?

We know the golfing dimensions we must fulfil to hit the ball straight and solid, and we know the starting set-up that gives us the best chance of meeting them. Now let's look at the movements we must make to maintain those all-important dimensions.

There are two objectives of the backswing, but both are not always clear to many golfers. One they obviously know, which is the creation of momentum – building power that can be released into the ball on the through-swing. The other they tend to miss, but it is extremely important. The second objective of having a certain type of backswing is *to get the golf club into a position from which it can be swung into the back of the ball square to the target.*

Let's look at each in turn.

In golf, both ends of the player must be fixed: his feet to the ground to provide a solid operating platform, and his head in one stable position to ensure that his swing arc remains constant. This being so, the only way he can create power is to coil the part in between, and that is exactly how the backswing does the job.

You create your power in golf – or the greater percentage of it – by turning the top half of your body against the resistance of your lower half, just as a coil-spring works. And it is not at all a complicated manoeuvre. Basically all you have to do is keep your head still, pivot your shoulders, and resist from the hips down. Consequent upon your shoulders turning, your arms will naturally swing the club back from the ball. When the weight of the clubhead begins to exert leverage on your wrists – as it passes hip height – they will naturally and automatically hinge or cock.

Power-wise, that's all there is to the backswing. How far you can hit the ball will largely depend upon how tight you can coil, top half against bottom half, and still keep everything under control. What you must avoid is forcing yourself beyond your natural limits. Ascertain what they are, in the physical sense, then be content to play within them, or practise and train to extend them. Always beware of over-extending yourself for the sake of power alone: it will lead to head

The correct backswing. The shoulders pivot against the resistance of the legs and hips as the hands and arms swing the club back and up and point it parallel to the original aim. Note that the start-back is a one-piece movement

movement, body swaying, ballet-dancing footwork and a whole host of errors that will wreck your swing dimensions. If you do want to increase your distance, work on clamping your feet to the ground, making your legs and knees resilient and your hips firm, turning rather than tilting your shoulders, a strong, smooth arm-swing, and a proper wrist-cock. Never worry about how far back the club goes; its

distance will be determined by your physical make-up, and you should make no artificial attempt to increase or decrease it.

Now let's look at the second objective of the backswing, getting the club into a position from which you can swing it squarely into the back of the ball along the target-line. (And let me remind you that a square hit from a slow-moving clubhead often covers more yards than a glancing blow from a jet-propelled club.)

To begin with, I want you to understand that we are still dealing with the basic golfing dimensions, in this case

the direction of the swing and the angle of the club's approach to the ball. You did your best to establish these correctly at address by your body alignment and posture, and your relationship to the clubface. You have now got to stay with what you established right through the backswing, so that you end up at the top with the two still in complete balance.

Here's how to go about it.

Start the swing with a smooth turn of your *right* shoulder *away* from the ball. Simultaneously with this *smooth* movement your arms will begin to swing the club, but be sure that they remain at this stage closely related to your shoulder-turn; allow your arms and the club (which still forms a straight extension of your arms) to *follow* the natural path dictated by your turning shoulders, rather than forcing them in some other direction.

As your shoulders turn, resist their pull in your legs, hips and feet. Keep your head still. Keep your left arm reasonably straight. Allow your right arm to bend at the elbow as it wishes.

You will find that almost immediately the clubhead starts to travel back from the ball, it moves 'inside' your target-line, and that it continues to

(Left) The slicer's backswing. He starts from an open address position, fails to turn his shoulders and picks the club up steeply with his hands and arms. *(Right)* The hooker. He starts from a closed address position and swings flatly around himself

move inside as your shoulders continue to turn. This is perfectly correct and natural, and is the only way you can maintain the swing plane you established at address. Under no circumstances try to force the clubhead 'straight back' from the ball, i.e., keep it artificially travelling back along the target-line. Equally, do not pull it more 'inside' than your shoulder turn is already taking it with an independent movement of your hands, wrists or arms. Just let your arms follow the turn

of your shoulders naturally as they swing the club up. In other words, by simply letting the club follow your shoulder-turn, remain at all points of the swing in the plane you established through your address position.

By the time your shoulders have turned through 90 degrees, your hips will have been pulled into a 45-degree

Opposite: Aim the club at the target at address, and maintain your direction of swing by aiming it parallel to the target-line at the top of the backswing

28

turn, but you will still be resisting hard from your feet to your waist. As your shoulder-turn nears completion, your arms and hands will have swung the club to somewhere around hip height, and the weight of the clubhead as it rises will be encouraging your wrists to hinge. Let them do so as the club goes up and over your shoulders.

Now, if you have come this far with a proper shoulder-turn, a resistant lower half, a still head and no independent manipulation of the club through your hands or wrists, the plane of your swing will still be as you established it at address. This in turn means that your angle of approach to the ball will be correct when you swing down.

You have, however, still to ensure that you are swinging in the right direction, so that when you swing down naturally, the clubhead will travel along the target-line for a few inches either side of the ball.

You will be thankful to know that this is one of the simplest operations in golf. All you have to do is point the club at your target as it reaches the top of the backswing. Simply make a conscious effort, as your swinging arms and cocking wrists complete the backswing, to bring the club on line – parallel to your target-line and pointing at your target.

Now, before we go on to the downswing, I want to explain that this description of the backswing is a detailed analysis of a fairly simple, fast and flowing movement, made necessary by the written medium. Not for a moment would I suggest that you actually try to play with a conscious step-by-step approach to the backswing, as I have broken it down here.

The way to tackle the job is to work on one facet at a time, on the practice ground or in the back garden, until everything fits together without conscious effort into a smooth, flowing movement.

4

The Downswing,
Hitting Area and Follow-through

Co-ordinating body and club action

The downswing is the most hazardous area of golf for a high percentage of people. They may have gripped correctly, aimed and stood correctly, and made a perfect backswing. Then, for some mysterious reason, it all evaporates. On their way down to the ball everything goes wrong. They have the utmost struggle both to contact the back of the ball solidly and to keep the clubhead facing and moving in the right direction.

The reason is simple. They fail properly to co-ordinate the two basic movements of the downswing, which are an unwinding of the hips, and a down-and-through swing of the arms, hands and golf club.

At the top of a good backswing, you will have achieved two things above anything else: wound or coiled yourself up, by turning your upper half against the resistance of your lower half; and swung the club on the correct line by swinging your arms and cocking your wrists in relation to your shoulder pivot. In other words, you will have generated power and charted direction.

The trick now is to release the first without destroying the second. It is the most difficult manoeuvre in golf, but within anyone's grasp who will practise regularly and intelligently.

Turning your upper half to the right creates a powerful reflex pull to the left in your lower half. It is by simply releasing this strong pull of the legs and hips towards the target that a golfer *always* initiates his downswing. The left knee slides or kicks back to the left, the right knee follows it, the weight goes with them, and the hips are pulled a little laterally across towards the target, and are then obliged to turn away or 'open' so that ultimately they have cleared a passage for the arms to swing past the body.

But here is where we come to the crunch. Although this hip slide and turn is vital, in terms of both power and direction, *it is only half the downswing story*. With it must always be combined *a proper down-and-through swing of the arm, hands and golf club*. Because, only if your arms and hands are bringing the club to the ball in strict

31

co-ordination with the turning of your hips, will you maintain right up until impact the golfing dimensions we have been at such pains to build into your game previously.

It is primarily because they are too hip conscious, or, less often, too hand conscious, that otherwise competent-looking golfers stumble at the last fence. All the current instruction books and most of the modern golf teachers stress that a golfer's hips must lead his downswing, and they are dead right. But what a lot of them forget to

mention is that, at the same time, he must *swing the club down to the ball with his arm.* I strongly believe that the work of the arms is the most neglected area in golf. We talk hands and we talk body, but it is the *arms* that make the actual golf swing. Swing them and your hands will work. Neglect them and you will have too much body action relative to your clubhead action.

As always in golf, what happens to the ball will tell you whether your own hip and arm-and-hand action are co-ordinated, and why not if they are not.

If you are slicing and/or topping, pulling or hitting the ball 'thin', it is a safe bet – assuming, of course, that your grip, set-up and backswing are

The correct downswing. The legs and hips clear the left side out of the way while the hands and arms swing the club down and through the ball

correct – that on the way down to the ball you have too much hip action relative to your arm swing. What usually happens here is that you start the downswing with a deliberate, conscious hip slide or twist towards the target, with no balancing thought of swinging your arms down simultaneously. The effect of this is to 'lock' your club to your shoulders. The hip turn pulls the shoulders around – out and over with the right shoulder, is the feeling – while the club is still high in the air. This throws your direction of swing from out-to-in across the target-line, steepens the angle of approach so that you cannot get into the back of the ball, and forces you to leave the club-

face open at impact. In other words, you are hitting 'too late' with your arms, hands and wrists, and 'too early' with your hips and shoulders. You are hitting the ball with your body, instead of the golf club.

If you saw a picture of yourself taken from the front half-way through the downswing, you would notice that your shoulders had followed your hip turn and were already open to the target – facing left of it. You would also see that there was hardly any 'daylight' between your hands and right shoulder – your hands and the club would be much too high in the air relative to the point of the downswing you had actually reached.

The cure for this fault – which afflicts 70 per cent of golfers – is simple. All you have to do is slow down or cut down your hip slide and/or turn, and simultaneously quicken or increase your downward arm-swing. When you hit solidly into the back of the ball and it starts straight on target, you have achieved the perfect blend, but you will only get it from assiduous and thoughtful practice.

More rare than the golfer who overdoes hip and body action in the downswing is the player who brings the club to the ball before his hip and leg movement has set up proper clearance for his arm-and-hand swing. He will be a hooker, a pusher, a fluffer and a 'heavy' hitter. Usually, he is a good player, with a lot of natural handspeed and an aggressive swing attitude.

What this player does is to swing his arms down as the first or dominating movement of the through-swing. This 'unlocks' the club from his body too quickly, and brings it down too soon, causing him to hit the ground behind the ball. Such a type of action also brings the club down very much inside the target-line, creating an in-to-out clubhead path at impact. Finally, because the player's hips haven't cleared a way for his arms to swing past his body – they haven't 'opened' enough – he is forced to roll his hands and wrists in the impact area, thereby committing the final sin and closing the clubface.

If you are this sort of golfer and you saw yourself on film, you would notice that halfway through the downswing your hips were still facing front, your right shoulder was still very much 'inside' your left shoulder (as it was at the top of the backswing), and that there was a lot of 'daylight' between your hands and shoulders, your hands being very low.

The cure again, with thoughtful practice, is simple. What you have to do is quicken or increase your hip turn – the initiation of the downswing by your lower half – while slowing or cutting down your arm-and-hand swing. In other words, you need to unwind 'earlier' with your body, and 'hit later' with the club. When the club contacts the back of the ball solidly, and it starts straight, you have achieved the perfect blend. Again, you'll only get it from study and practice.

What does need to be stressed here is that the downswing is the most difficult movement in golf to master. Learning to grip the club, set-up to the ball and make a good backswing is not hard with some intelligent application. But considerable practice and perseverance is necessary to arrive at the correct down- and through-swing, even if you have natural talent.

I am often asked about the follow-

Opposite: Backview of the correct downswing and its result, the follow-through. To hit straight, solid shots, you must combine downswing hip action with a strong armswing that will apply the clubhead to the ball 'in time'

through in golf: what is its significance? My answer is that the follow-through is extremely useful in determining what has gone before – in analysing faults. It's actual shape will help to show the type of swing a golfer is using, and his relationship to the three vital golfing dimensions at impact, just as the flight of the ball does. But that is all. If a golfer arrives at impact with his clubface square to the target, his swing-line coinciding with his target-line, and a good angle of approach, his follow-through will be correct – it can't, mechanically, be anything else.

So much, then, for the basic dimensions and techniques of the golf swing. I shall be coming back to them throughout the remainder of these lessons, but now let's move on to some specific shots and playing situations.

5
Club Variations
14 clubs – but one swing

There are fourteen clubs in a full golfing set, but this does not mean – as some golfers seem to think – that you must have fourteen different swings. Basic playing techniques remain unaltered, whatever club you have in your hand, any time you want to hit the ball straight to the target.

You start by aiming the clubface squarely where you want to go, then align yourself squarely to the clubface. From that carefully planned set-up, you make two body turns and a hand-and-arm swing in a way that will meet the vital golfing dimensions. Such modifications as are necessary between the driver and the wedge derive, almost automatically, from the shape of the clubs themselves, rather than from any deliberate manoeuvres on your part.

With the driver, for instance, you will naturally stand at your farthest point from the ball, because it is the longest club in the bag. Likewise, you will stand with your feet at their widest apart to give you a solid base for your biggest swing. You will also stand at your most erect – back straight, head

high, and only a slight bend at the waist and knees. All these factors are dictated by the club itself, and they will naturally create your flattest or most shallow swing plane, so that the club can make a wide arc and hit solidly into the back of the ball by following a shallow, sweeping path in the impact area.

On the other hand, with a wedge you will stand at your closest point to the ball, simply because it is the shortest club in the bag. You will not be making as big a body turn either way as you do with a driver, so your feet will be closer together. To get the club behind the ball you will have to lean over it more, with a bigger bend at the waist and knees and your head at a lower level. As a result of all these factors, your swing plane will automatically be at its steepest – the club will follow a more upright path, facilitating a sharply downward rather than a sweeping clubhead trajectory in the hitting area.

It is always advisable, so far as is possible, to let these modifications take care of themselves, and to concentrate

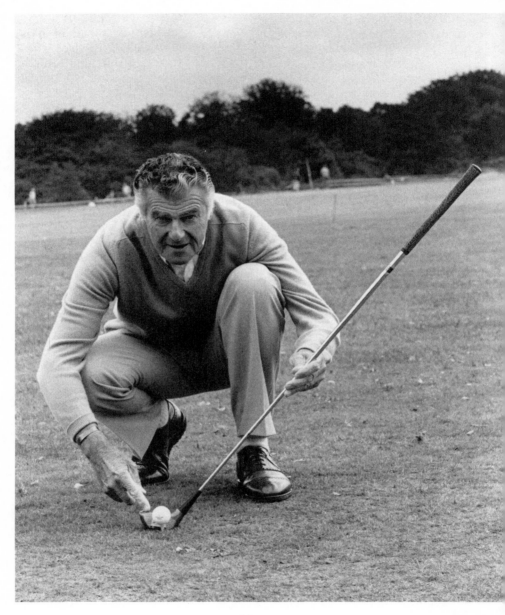

on making a fundamentally good set-up and swing. There are, however, a few points about club variations which it is worth underlining to help you to set your sights correctly, and to clear up a few common misconceptions.

The first thing to remember is that with a driver you want to hit the ball *forward* as strongly as possible. The driver's straight face demands that you do so, and its effectiveness will be greatly diminished if your angle of approach in the hitting area is at all steep. Even if you make a solid contact while coming into the ball steeply, the downward angle of the blow will serve to increase the backspin you put on the ball, and the more backspin, the quicker the ball loses its forward thrust.

Opposite and below: Tee the ball for a driver so that half of it shows above the grounded club. This way you are encouraged to hit it forward with a sweeping action so as to decrease distance-losing backspin

This is why, with a driver, we tee the ball up high − so that half of it is projecting above the driver face when the club is laid on the ground behind. So long as we then make a sweeping approach − the club travelling low to the ground in the impact area − we are able to contact the ball at the bottom of the club's arc, and thereby produce minimum backspin and maximum forward thrust.

So do not, if you want distance, tee the ball low then hit down on it. Tee it high and sweep the club solidly into its back, without letting the clubhead touch the ground at all. Swish it away 'clean' and try to leave the tee-peg in the ground.

Although with the fairway woods, the ball must be hit at the bottom of the swing arc, or fractionally before it, you still need to use a driver-type set-up and swing − a flattish plane and a sweeping arc in the hitting area. So, once again, stand tall from your hips to your shoulders, and comfortably away from the ball with your feet forming a solid base.

With the irons the shorter the club and the more lofted it is, the nearer you stand to the ball, the closer together your feet move, and the more you lean over from the waist. This is not only for anatomical reasons, but to sharpen or steepen the angle of the swing, and thereby produce an increasingly down-ward hit which imparts the backspin that controls the ball's flight, distance and stopping power.

With the long irons, you are still

using almost a sweeping action, very comparable to the fairway woods. With the medium irons, your swing has become a little more upright, and you are therefore hitting more 'down and through' the ball. With the short irons, your swing has adopted its most upright plane – it is as near to being vertical, or straight up and down from the ball, as it ever gets. But if you set-up properly, you should not have to think consciously about these angles – they will take care of themselves.

One thing that puzzles many golfers is that they hit short- and medium-iron shots fairly straight, yet, with the same swing, badly slice tee-shots. This often

You stand further away with the longer irons, and consequently the swing is less upright

leads them to try all sorts of complicated compensations, most of which only further confuse the issue.

The fact is that the golfer with this problem is using a slice grip, set-up and swing for *all* his shots, but the type of spin imparted to the ball by the lofted clubs largely disguises his faults. Here's how.

Because of its straight face, the driver contacts the *back centre* of the ball, but is being dragged across the ball from out-to-in. Consequently, a great deal of sidespin is imparted, which quickly overcomes the weak forward thrust resulting from a glancing blow. When the golfer uses a medium or short iron, however, the greater loft on the clubface allows it to get down to the *bottom back* of the ball, even with an out-to-in swing-line. This type of contact produces backspin rather than sidespin, and therefore, largely nullifies the slice.

So, don't kid yourself. The straight-faced clubs are the ones that tell you what you are *really* doing, and it is your effectiveness with these that should always be uppermost in your mind if you want to be a good player.

6
Revision
The classic case of Joe Bloggs

One of the longest hitters of all time, and one of the greatest amateur golfers ever, was an Irishman called Jimmy Bruen. His feats are legendary, especially 'over the water'. But if you had seen Bruen swing without a ball, you would hardly have believed the game he played was golf. His action, which included an enormous looping movement, seemed to defy every swing theory known to man.

Most golfers will have seen Arnold Palmer and Jack Nicklaus, on film if not in the flesh. Palmer's wrists at the top of the backswing are in a position that very few teachers would recommend, and at one time he virtually fell over after every drive due to the way he went through the ball. Nicklaus's right elbow, at the top of his swing, is well away from the 'orthodox' position. His action is nothing like Palmer's, nor is Palmer's like Ben Hogan's, nor Hogan's like Henry Cotton's.

How is it, then, that these golfers – and many more like them who seem to have some major swing flaw – play such great golf? The answer is simple:

whatever they do on the way up from and the way down to the ball, they are 'right' at impact. At the moment it contacts the ball, the face of the club is square to the target, it is swinging in the right direction, and it is moving at the right angle. Each in his own way has learned not 'how to swing a golf club', but how to make a golf swing fulfil those three vital objectives.

If club players could only force themselves to tackle the game this way, they would be very much better golfers and happier people. For this is the only 'secret' of golf. The criterion of a golf swing is neither its beauty nor its ugliness as an athletic movement, but simply its effectiveness as a means of getting the ball from A to B. And a player's effectiveness in getting the ball from A to B is dependent entirely on how well or poorly he can meet the game's basic mechanical requirements. What it 'looks like' is of no significance if it works repetitively.

Unfortunately, few golfers either appreciate or accept the fact that there are no absolute rights about the golf

(Top) This is how your grip must return the clubface at impact if you are to hit the ball solidly and fly it straight. Grip errors that leave the clubface open *(middle)* are the root causes of slicing. Conversely, a grip which presents the clubface closed *(above)* leads to hooking

swing as a *movement*. They seek 'the secret', and because there has always been in golf so much accent on playing methods, they look for it in swing techniques. So, right from the start, the vast majority put effect before cause in all their golfing efforts. And, even more sadly, most go on doing so for the rest of their playing days.

The average handicap of perhaps fifteen million men golfers throughout the world is probably about eighteen. Considering the physical and mental equipment of most of the people concerned, I regard that as being an extraordinarily poor mark. Golf is a difficult game, but I think any moderately fit, moderately sane male should be capable of knocking round the normal sort of course in eighty shots or a couple over. But they can't, and to see exactly what stops most of them, let's have a look at a typical case history.

Joe Bloggs took up golf when he gave up cricket. He is passably athletic, passably well-co-ordinated, passably intelligent. The chum who introduced him to the golf club has fixed him up with some gear and given him a few tips. He's had a few swishes in a quiet corner. Out he goes on the course for his first proper game.

Joe has been shown broadly how to hold the club, but he hasn't been told why, beyond perhaps 'Because that's the way good players do it'. His natural tendency will be to grip the club with his hands weakly positioned. On top of that he has not, of course, yet had time to build any golfing muscle or flexibility in his hands, wrists and arms. The inevitable outcome will be that, whatever his actual swing is like, when he hits the ball his clubface will be open. (He needn't be ashamed; most beginners are the same.)

Because of Joe's open clubface at impact, his first few shots on the course will go to the right. Very soon this tendency to favour right field will become both tiresome and embarrassing, especially if it involves a lot of ball-hunting. Eventually Joe will begin to get desperate. He has no knowledge of golf technique at this stage, but he knows that somehow he has to hit the thing more to the left. So instinct takes over, and here Joe makes a move that will more than likely set the seal of doom on his whole golfing career.

His ball, even when well struck on occasion, has been going to the right. So in double-quick time Joe does the *natural* thing: he leaves his grip and his swing alone (he doesn't really know how to change them), and simply aims himself more to the left. 'That'll stop it,' he says to himself, and he's right. All of a sudden Joe's ball stops going straight into the woods on the right, and starts instead to the left. But – and here's the wonderful thing for Joe – it doesn't go into trouble on the left. Halfway through its flight it bends to the right again, and finishes in the fairway. 'Got it!' says our delighted Joe. 'Good shot, Joe!' say his chums, delighted they're not going on yet another jungle expedition. And suddenly Joe can play – at least, well enough to get round. And suddenly another habitual slicer has joined the frustrated millions. . .

Of course, if Joe is really keen on the game, his initial delight at being able simply to get round the course will soon evaporate. The limitations of his slice will become apparent as his experience increases, and will move him to look for some stronger and more reliable type of shot. At this point he reaches another cross-roads. If he follows the small minority, he will head for a competent professional, take a series of lessons, and practice assiduously what he is told to do. If he joins the majority, he will begin to examine swing theory on his own account. He will listen to friends, analyse what good players try to do, study books and magazines – with particular reference to 'stopped' action pictures – and, on the basis of all this, he will experiment every time he goes on the golf course (always to play, of course, never to practise). 'There has *got* to be a secret,' he will say to himself, and his search for it will be diligent and relentless. He will become, in time, a master theoretician, versed in every nuance of swing technique from hand-pronation to hip-slide, from right-side thrust to reverse wrist-cock. Unfortunately, he will, as like as not, remain a long-handicapper.

For, despite all Joe's mighty efforts to become a fine golfer, he never gets to the root of the matter. By working on his swing, without knowing how to relate it to what the ball does, he has the cart squarely in front of the horse.

Your swing must be in the direction of the target. Body alignment and posture at address *(left)* are vital. The backswing must maintain your swing direction and plane; you achieve this *(right)* by turning your shoulders and pointing the club parallel to the target

The result is inevitable: he does a lot of work but continues to stand still.

What the Joes of golf really need are some lessons from professionals who say *why* before they show *how;* who get the picture over mentally before they start shoving things around physically. If I have had any success at teaching golf, it is essentially because I have always tried to explain why I am asking the pupil to do something in a certain way – and because golfers are mainly intelligent people. Once you tell people what they are *really* trying to do with a golf club, it is surprising how many of them can do it quite easily.

So, if you are seriously bent on improvement, I must ask you once again never to lose sight of what you are really trying to do.

Your club must be square to the target at impact, and this is controlled by your grip and aim. If the ball is bending in the air, your grip or your initial clubface aim is wrong and you will need to experiment until the ball

46

continues to fly in the direction in which it starts. When that happens, your grip is correct *for you*.

Next, your club must be travelling in the right direction, which means along the target-line, at impact. This is 90 per cent controlled by the alignment of your shoulders at address. They must be parallel to the target-line, not facing left or right of your target. Check constantly that they are so positioned – get someone to look at you carefully from behind at address any time the ball does not start straight at the target.

Finally, your angle of approach must enable your club to swing solidly into the back of the ball. This is controlled by your swing plane, which you establish by your body posture at address. Do not stand like a guardsman; do not bend as though you've just spotted a sixpence on the ground. Adjust your posture by how solidly you are meeting the ball.

And one final very important point. If you have been doing it all wrong for a long time past, you won't perfect the new systems in a matter of minutes. You may very well feel uncomfortable, miss a lot of shots at first, get tired and disillusioned.

But, if you want to be a good player, all I can say is: make sure you start your swing from the proper position, stay with the game, give it a proper go. You have nothing to lose but some handicap strokes.

7

Chipping and Pitching

The short cuts to lower scores

Whether you are loosing off with a driver at a big, wide par-five fairway, or playing a delicate little pitch to a tiny, fast-running green, the principles of the golf stroke remain the same. In fact, the nearer you get to the hole, the less your margin for error, and therefore the more accurate must be your clubface alignment, direction of swing and angle of attack on the ball. But, although the basic mechanics we have been discussing still apply on the very short shots, they also involve a number of special playing techniques. So let's now look at these in detail.

I mentioned earlier that it is always desirable in golf to have a clear mental picture of the shot you are about to hit. With all the little shots, being able to 'see' the behaviour of the ball in the mind's-eye at the planning stage is absolutely essential. It is the only way you can positively determine the type of shot you want to play, and thereby decide which club, used with which particular technique, will do the job for you.

Some golfers do not appreciate that there is a clear distinction between a chip-shot and a pitch-shot, and therefore tend to use only one club for all their short approaches and play largely by intuition or instinct. If that works for you, well and good. But for most it is rather a haphazard system, and there are invariably golfing situations where it will come to grief. To my mind, it is better to know the specific clubs and techniques that produce certain effects, and to be able to produce them at will.

A chip is the shot used when there are no hazards intervening between a player and the hole, and there is plenty of green upon which he can run the ball. The idea is to loft the ball into the air for the minimum distance and roll it along the ground for most of its journey. This kind of shot is played usually from just off the green, and

Opposite: (top left) The set-up for a chip shot. From here the club is swung back slightly on the 'inside' with the hands and arms *(top right and bottom left)*, then goes from the inside straight through the ball to the target *(bottom right)*

every iron club in the bag can be used, depending on the relative amount of loft and run required. If, for example, your ball was just off the green at the front and the pin was right at the back, you might use a five-iron, just to pop the ball over the few feet of fringe grass and make it run four-fifths of its way to the hole. If, on the other hand, you were twenty yards short of the green, you would need a more lofted club to loft the ball to the putting surface before it started to run – say an eight-

iron. One of the great arts in chipping is to know what each club will do for you, then to make the correct choice.

Pitching is the exact opposite of chipping. The idea here is to loft the ball to the hole-side almost entirely through the air, stopping it as close as possible to where it lands. Obviously the shot is played when some sort of hazard intervenes between the player and his target, or when the pin location doesn't allow for roll. A pitch of this type can cover anything between a hundred yards and a few feet, and it is always played with the most lofted clubs, normally the pitching-wedge, sand-wedge or nine-iron.

Backspin is largely what stops a golf

Playing a short pitch shot with the wedge. Weight on left side, upright hand-and-arm swing with plenty of wrist action, hands leading the clubhead as it slides down and under the ball

ball when it lands, so a main objective of the technique you use in chipping is to minimise backspin. In pitching, on the other hand, you will do all you can to impart maximum backspin to the ball.

You start to play a chip – as you do every other golf shot – by aiming the clubface where you want the ball to go. So, even though it is only a short and easy-looking shot, *do not* plonk your feet down any old place, then just drop the clubhead behind the ball. Take your grip and aim the clubhead first, then begin to take your stance relative to the clubhead aim.

There are two essential points to work upon in preparing to chip, beyond the standard preparations for a golf shot. The first is to place your weight predominantly on your left side – 'leaning' on your left leg would aptly describe it. The second is to ensure that your hands are 'leading' the club – that they are about three inches *ahead* of the ball when you are in your final address position.

For the rest, try to be comfortable. Do not crouch or stand to attention. Let your arms hang comfortably from your shoulders, just far enough away from your body to give them free passage. There will be no conscious body action, so place your feet comfortably close together. Stand so that you are slightly open to the hole with your

feet but keep your shoulders square; this will allow for your arms to swing the club easily past your body and straight through towards the target. Place your head over the ball, and keep your eyes on the *back* of the ball, the bit you intend to hit.

Now, if you have set yourself up correctly, you will have achieved two things in particular: first, you will have aimed the clubface where you want to hit the ball; second, you will have put yourself in such a position that you will strike the ball just before the club reaches the bottom of its arc – in other words, you will be hitting very slightly *downwards* into the ball, not scooping up at it as so many golfers do when they try to chip.

Before you swing, finally check your aim. You will have picked a spot where you want the ball to land in picturing the shot. Check that the clubface is pointing to that spot, swivelling your head and glancing from the club to the landing spot, *without turning your whole upper body.*

You are now almost ready to go, but before you do you must make one final – and vital – decision, namely the strength of hit you are going to apply to send the ball the required distance. This will be controlled by the *length of your backswing,* not by muscular force. As your final act of preparation, mentally assess how long a backswing you will need to give the ball the required loft and roll, and stay with that thought from there on. Among the commonest causes of poor chipping are taking too short a backswing for the required distance, then jabbing the club at the ball in an effort to hit it harder, and taking too long a backswing then decelerating the club just before impact. Always make a few practice swings to get the feel of the distance – you will notice the pro's do.

Finally, the swing. You have set-up with your hands ahead of the ball. From there simply swing the club back with your arms, so that the club goes back barely inside the target-line. Once you have got it back far enough like that to be able to hit the ball the required distance without rushing or jerking, simply reverse the process. Keeping your hands leading the clubhead, and your arms pulling your hands and club along smoothly, swing the club down to and through the ball from slightly inside the target-line. Maintain an *even* pace throughout; with this approach the club will go through straight to the target. Try to ensure that the length of your follow-through roughly matches the length of your backswing. Given the right set-up, and good pace, it is essentially a simple movement.

In chipping, you use a standard technique, allowing the loft of the clubface to determine the relative flight and roll of the ball. In pitching, some slight variations in technique are necessary to increase or decrease the club's in-built loft, depending on circumstances. For a fairly long pitch into heavy wind, for instance, you might need to deloft the club a little to prevent the ball soaring and falling short. You would do so by playing it well back towards the right foot, with the clubface slightly closed or 'hooded' and the hands well in front at address and impact. For a short, very high shot over a bunker – a lob, almost – you would do the opposite: place the ball forward in relation to the feet, open the clubface, and keep the hands level with the ball at address and impact. Common sense and experience must be applied to all golf shots, but pitching in particular.

In chipping, the basic idea is to hit the ball *forward* with minimum backspin, and this is achieved by leaving out conscious wrist-action and thereby creating a wide and shallow swing arc – rather like a long putt. In pitching, exactly the opposite obtains. We want to get the ball *up* and give it maximum backspin. This necessitates a narrow or steep swing-arc, and a pronounced downward as well as a forward hit. We get such an effect from plenty of wristwork.

You aim and set yourself up for a short pitch very much as you do for a chip, except that you vary the placement of the ball and the angle of the clubface according to the amount of height and forward trajectory you require. The big difference is in the swing. Whereas in the chip there is little wrist-action, in pitching it is essential that your wrists hinge or cock very early in the backswing, *and that they stay cocked until late in the downswing.* Only in this way can you slide the club down and through the bottom back of the ball, and thereby give it heavy backspin and rapid height.

Most club golfers who pitch poorly do so because they cannot make themselves hit the ball *down* to make it rise – they scoop up at it with their weight back on the right foot at address and impact, too long an arm-swing, and insufficient wrist-action. If you are one of these, get your weight on your left side, and, if you have followed the correct address procedure, when you cock your wrists the club will swing up slightly on the inside, from where it is easy to hit down and through to the target. Judge your distance by the length of your backswing, always keep your hands leading the ball at impact (and you can only do that if you've cocked your wrists), and swing down crisply. The follow-through will normally be shorter than the back-swing, because we hit 'to' the left wrist, not 'past' it.

Few golfers can ever hope to emulate top professionals with the woods and long irons, but, with intelligent practice, all can master chipping and pitching. And therein, of course, lies the shortest of all short-cuts to lower scores.

8
Putting

Help only if you need it

If you are a consistently good putter, my advice to you would be either to skip this chapter, or, if you are so inquisitive that you must read it, not to let it influence your own proven method. Anything – and I mean *anything* – that really works on the greens is worth holding on to!

But if you are not a good putter, stay with me. I think I can offer you a few thoughts that might result in considerable improvement.

The first thing I want to do is to bring clearly to the forefront of your mind once again exactly what you are trying to do. It is the same with a putter as it is with a driver or a wedge: you are trying to hit straight through the ball with a square clubface. If you can combine that, in this case, fairly simple physical manoeuvre with good judgement of line and distance, you will be bound to hole a lot of putts.

The first priority in putting therefore – as with every golf shot – is to assess the line and the strength of hit, and get everything organised so that you can move the ball accordingly. Reading greens is a matter of intuition and experience, which I will have to leave to you. What I do want you to do, *always*, is to properly aim the club and yourself relative to the line once you have established it. A lot of golfers have difficulty even at this opening stage. They have a putt with, say, a six-inch borrow from the right. Instead of aiming themselves and the clubface six inches to the right, they point everything at the hole, then try to manoeuvre the ball to the right with the actual stroke itself. That is never a sound putting system. You must establish the *starting* line of every putt, then aim the club and yourself squarely to that. Remember that, in terms of starting the ball – or of impact dimensions, to put it another way – every putt is dead straight.

Bringing the clubface square to the target is controlled in putting, as it is in every other shot, by your grip. In the long shots the hands must hold the club in the way we have previously described to cope with a big swing arc and transmit a lot of power; but these

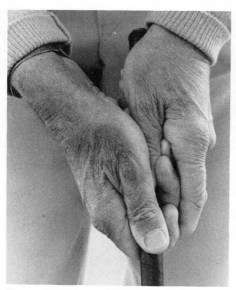

The most popular putting grip. Back of left hand and palm of right facing the target, thumbs straight down the shaft, and forefinger of left hand overlapping fingers of right hand. It all serves to keep the clubface square throughout

Conventional Vardon overlapping grip, but with the back of the left hand and palm of right facing the target

factors do not enter into putting, and therefore the grip becomes much simplified. In a nutshell, the best putting grip for keeping the club face square is one in which the back of the left hand and the palm of the right hand exactly face the target – in other words, the palms are in parallel with the clubface. Beyond that, how you actually hold the club is a matter of personal preference although the reverse overlapping grip – with the forefinger of the left hand wrapped around the fingers of the right

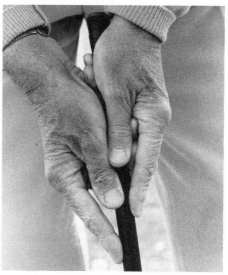

Right: Again palms opposite but with both index fingers extended down the shaft

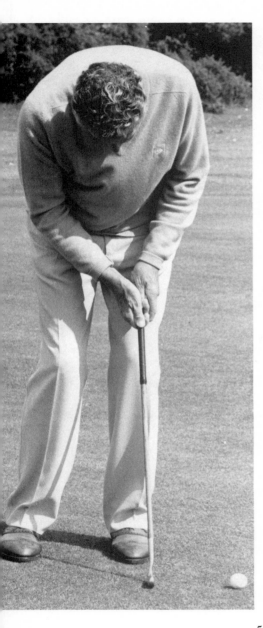

hand – is probably the most popular of all the scores of grip styles used by good putters.

Once we are certain that our grip will maintain a square clubface, our next concern is swinging it in the right direction. And here on the greens, as well as through the green, we give ourselves the best chance of doing that if we ourselves stand square to where we intend to go. So it's back to the railway tracks, or narrow-gauge tram-lines if you prefer. The ball is on the far one, which represents your target-line. You are standing on the near one, and you position yourself as parallel to it as is humanly possible, right from the feet to the shoulders. Subject to that alignment, your actual posture is again a matter of comfort and personal pre-ference, but most good putters bend from the neck and waist, with the feet fairly close together and solidly planted, and the head exactly over the ball so that the eyes are looking straight down at it.

So we have clearly established the line and squarely aimed the clubface and ourselves relative to it, just as with any other golf shot. We come now to the stroke itself, and here's where I think I can help a lot of ailing putters.

For much of the time I played tournament golf, I was a relatively poor putter, and one of the reasons, I now realise, was that I had let myself

The putting set-up. Everything from feet to shoulders square to the starting line of the putt, feet solidly planted, eyes directly over the ball

be influenced by some of the scores of clichés that attach to putting 'method'. The two most damaging in my case were 'Take the putter straight back along the line', and 'Keep the putter head low to the ground'. For years I tried like fury to do both. Only in recent years have I appreciated that it is virtually impossible to do the first on any putt over about six feet and consistently make a square and solid strike; and that it is totally impossible to do both together and still make an easy, fluid and natural movement of the putter head.

On a very short putt, where the club moves back no more than two or three inches, obviously one can swing straight back and straight through. But, outside that range, hitting straight through, with the club staying close to the turf throughout the stroke, necessitates going back *inside* to some degree. It is the same as any golf shot: the only direction from which you can swing the putter squarely through the ball at impact is from the '*inside*'. And, if you are a poor putter, this is what you should consciously try to do on all but the shortest putts. Don't neglect the preliminaries. Aim the clubface squarely along the line, stand square to the line yourself, rest the putter flush on the ground. Then swing it back slightly *inside* the target line. The visual impression will be that you are closing or 'hooding' the putter face, but this will not be the case if you stand still and don't roll or twist your wrists – the putter face will, in fact, remain square

The putting stroke. Club swung back low to ground slightly inside the target-line with the face square, then returned along the same line and straight through the ball

relative to the ball's starting direction. And, most important of all, when you return the putter to the ball, swing it along the same *from-the-inside* line. In other words, make your stroke from inside to straight-through the ball, remembering that, on a very long putt, the club would eventually move 'inside' again on the follow-through.

Pulling the ball to the left is the result

of trying to swing straight back along the target-line, which invariably leads to an out-to-in hit. The converse, pushing putts to the right, results from taking the same sort of swing-line with the clubface open. The putter again comes back across the line from out-to-in, and the open clubface produces a cutting or chopping effect. Both these faults are quickly cured by adopting an inside-to-straight-through swing-line.

You can physically make your putting stroke in one of three ways: (1) a direct hinging or breaking of the wrists from the address position, with little or no movement of the hands and arms; (2) a solid-wristed movement in which the hands, arms and club act as a single stroking unit; (3) a combination of the foregoing. All can be very effective, and if one goes off it is always worth trying another.

What has to be watched all the time, whatever type of stroke you use, is that you contact the ball with the clubhead smoothly accelerating. Many more putts are missed because of bad distance than bad direction. One major cause of this is decelerating the putter before impact, usually because of too long or too sloppy a backswing. The other, less common, is trying to do too much with too little backswing, then jabbing at the ball as the clubhead comes into it.

Having decided your line, aim the club correctly, then stand correctly. From that set-up, try to swing the putter straight through the ball *on line*, thinking mainly about the strength of hit you must apply to move the ball to the hole.

9
Trouble Shots
The art of cutting your losses

How well a golfer can get out of trouble depends largely on how well he can use the strongest weapon in his armoury – his brain. And the more difficult the spot he is in, the harder he must think before he strikes. Unfortunately, many golfers in trouble apply muscle first and intellect a remorseful second.

You need to think about three things whenever your ball lands somewhere unpleasant. First, whether you are playing match or medal, you must consider the immediate competitive situation. Can you afford to gamble, or should you play safe at all costs? Does everything rest upon the next shot, or just one hole or stroke? You know how you will react if you bring off a miracle; think also on what will happen to your composure and confidence if you don't.

Second, you must think about your physical limitations. *Can* you actually play the shot that you would like to? Are you good enough, swinging well enough, strong enough?

Third, you must think about *how* to play the shot you eventually decide

upon. Trouble shots require special techniques. They need to be thought out beforehand and clearly planted in the mind before you so much as take the club from the bag.

I can't help you with numbers one and two, but I can be of assistance with number three.

Basically, trouble means rough of various types, and in getting out of it you will have one of two objectives: hitting the green, or getting enough distance to be sure of hitting the green with your next shot. Let's look at the two techniques involved.

You are 150 yards from the green in fairly long grass, but with a not impossible lie for a well-lofted iron. There is a bunker between you and the pin. Because of this hazard, and because you know the ball runs more when hit from rough, you need height as well as distance.

The first thing you do with a shot of this type is to open the clubface as you address the ball, first to help you get height, and secondly to offset the tendency of the grass to close the clubface

Achieving height from rough requires a steep backswing with plenty of wrist action. The hips should clear on the through-swing to keep the clubface open through the ball

as it wraps around the club hosel at impact. However, if you hit the ball with the clubface open, using a normal through-to-the-target swing-line, the ball will go to the right. So, to offset this, you make a second address adjustment, which is to open your shoulders – align them left of the target – thus balancing the open clubface. You have, in fact, set-up for a slice: your out-to-in swing-line will be balanced by the open clubface, giving you a straight but higher shot.

With any shot from rough, a prime

objective is to minimise the amount of grass that gets between the clubface and the ball at impact. By setting yourself open, you have already established a steep out-to-in swing path. You steepen it even more on the backswing, by taking the club straight *up* from the ball with a strong, free armswing and plenty of wrist-cock, but not very much body turn. And here comes the crunch. You *must* start the downswing by clearing your hips out of the way, and keep them turning – opening towards the hole – right through the shot, so that your arms can get freely past your body. Only by doing that will you be able to swing the club steeply down into the ball with the face open.

Getting distance from rough. Clubface slightly hooded *(bottom right)*, ball well back and weight on left leg at address; steep backswing; sharp downswing into back of ball with hands always leading clubhead, driving the ball forward to produce maximum roll and distance

If your hips don't move smartly, your wrists will uncock too early, flattening the bottom of the swing, increasing your contact with the grass behind the ball, and forcing you to close the clubface – a fatal state of affairs in rough.

So, to summarise, open your shoulders and the clubface at address, swing *up* steeply with your arms and wrists, and keep your hips moving as you swing your arms sharply down into the back of the ball. Use this technique with any shot from rough where you have a reasonable chance of reaching the green with any iron up to a five, or

the four- and five-woods. Use it also when you are in really deep trouble and are trying simply to get back into play by the shortest route.

Now let's tackle the other problem, getting maximum distance in order to be able to reach the green with the following shot.

Imagine that you have just topped your tee-shot on a par-four, and are in nasty rough 380 yards from the green

– too bad a spot for a four-wood. You need to move the ball at least 170 yards up the fairway to have any chance of 'greening' your third shot.

The club you want here is a medium-iron – the four, five or six, depending on your lie – and you need to play it in such a way that you get the type of flight that will give you plenty of roll and thus gain distance. Once again, the set-up is all-important. Start by hooding or shutting the clubface slightly, then take your stance with the ball very much back towards your right foot and your weight two-thirds on your left leg. This will set your hands well ahead of the ball and keep your shoulders square.

Once again, you want to minimise the amount of grass that gets between the clubface and the ball. So, as in the other type of shot from rough, you must make a steep attack on the back of the ball. Swing the club up sharply with your hands, wrists and arms, making sure not to open the clubface, then drive it forcefully down into the back of the ball, taking your divot well in front of where the ball lay.

This is not an elegant shot – a hooded-face smash straight down on the back of the ball – but is most effective when the object is simply to move the ball the maximum distance back into play. You will have little follow-through as such, but if you can catch the ball fairly clean with the clubface hooded it will whistle out low, run a very long way on landing, and probably allow you to salvage a bogey if not a par. There will be a tendency to hook this shot, so aim to the right a little at address.

On many trouble shots, the problem is not just the stuff in which the ball is lying, but obstacles like trees around or over which it must be flighted. Such situations are not as difficult as they sometimes seem if you can draw upon a good knowledge of shot-making mechanics.

For instance, to deliberately slice the ball is extremely easy with a straight-faced club and becomes progressively harder the more loft the club possesses. Conversely, to hook the ball with a well-lofted club is not difficult, but gets harder the straighter the face. You should weigh up these factors carefully whenever there is an obstacle in your way.

Suppose, for example, that a high tree stands exactly on the line between you and the green. The green is 150 yards away and you are sixty yards behind the tree. You have the choice of three shots. You can try to hit the ball straight over the top of the tree, you can attempt to slice it round the tree from left-to-right, or you can try to hook it from right-to-left. What should you do? It would depend on your lie, and the state of your game.

If you had a fair lie, and felt you could get good height, you might go for the straight shot, positioning the ball well forward, keeping your hands level with it at address, and using plenty of wrist-action on both the backswing and through-swing – wrist-action produces height. If you lacked confidence about achieving enough height and distance, or the lie was not encouraging, but you were a natural hooker, you would probably go for the right-to-left shot. You would then take one *less* club than for an equivalent fairway shot, perhaps a seven-iron instead of a six-iron; aim the clubface and your shoulders well right of target with the ball fairly well back and your hands ahead; make a good shoulder turn in the backswing to maintain your in-to-out swingline; and hit strongly and *early* with your arms, wrists, hands and clubhead.

If the lie was bad, or the competitive situation was tight, or you weren't playing particularly well, or you were a natural slicer, you would definitely go for the left-to-right shot, which in the last analysis is the easy A-to-B shot from rough. You would take one *more* club than for an equivalent distance from the fairway – remember, you need a straight-faced club to help you slice the ball. You would open the clubface and yourself liberally at address, and swing the club steeply up and down with your hands and arms along the open swing-line established by your shoulders. You would then concentrate on keeping your hips going through the shot, and bringing the clubface sharply down and across the back of the ball.

If you can't swing your normal way round because of an obstruction, try turning a lofted iron nose down and swing the other way round. It's a way of at least moving the ball clear of trouble, but don't be too ambitious

So long as you kept your hips and arms moving, which would stop you closing the clubface at impact, the ball would start left and cut around the tree to the right and back on to the target.

Never be afraid, if you are in trouble, to make up or contrive a recovery shot if the percentages of saving a stroke seem in your favour. If you are close up against an obstacle and can't swing right-handed (or left-handed if you are a southpaw), turn a broad-bladed iron over so that its nose is pointing at the ground, and swing at the ball the other way round. It's possible to 'stun' the ball along the ground 100 yards or more like this. If you are close up against a wall with no room to swing, hit the ball at the wall and simply bounce it back into play. If you are under a bush and can't afford a pick and drop, try 'putting' the ball out.

Arnold Palmer has said that 'if you can see it, you can hit it, and if you can hit it, you can hole it'. I don't go all the way with that, but the basic sentiment is admirable. So long as you properly weigh up the odds, assess your own physical limitations, and have a good knowledge of the mechanical whys and wherefores of trouble shots, you can nearly always cut your losses at golf.

10

Sloping Lies

Up, down, above and below

Coping with sloping lies is largely a matter of modifying your stance and set-up to the ball so that you are still able to meet the vital golfing dimensions at impact. On top of that, you need to know what effects sloping ground have on the flight of the ball, and how to adjust your aim and club selection accordingly. Let's look at the four basic 'angles' in detail.

Uphill lie

If the ground was going uphill towards your target and you took a normal vertical stance, you would, in fact, be set-up to swing the club straight into the hillside. But you want, as always, to swing it *through* the ball, and the easy way to ensure that you can do that is to take your stance so that you are parallel to the slope. Simply take your normal address posture, then tilt everything to the right enough to let you swing down the slope in the backswing and up it in the through-swing. Place your hands level with the ball, 'dropping' your right shoulder as necessary to bring your shoulders parallel with the slope.

With this type of set-up your weight throughout the shot will be predominantly on your right side, and this will make it very easy for you to hook the ball. So aim a little right of target at the outset to be on the safe side. Also, remember that playing from an uphill lie increases height and reduces distance, so always take ample club – at least one more than you would from a level fairway lie.

Downhill lie

A downhill lie presents a much more difficult shot than an uphill lie, but exactly the same sort of common-sense swing principles apply.

Obviously if we took a normal vertical stance on ground running away from us, we'd tend to catch the ground on the backswing, and would certainly hit into it before we could get to the ball on the downswing. For this reason we again modify our set-up to suit the ground angle, tilting everything to the left until our shoulders are parallel to the slope and we can follow it with the clubhead in the backswing and through-swing.

When the ball is above your feet, you stand tall, swing as flatly as the slope dictates, and aim to the right to allow for the almost inevitable hook

With the ball below your feet, you must lean over and swing on an upright plane predominantly with your hands and arms. The ball will usually slice, so aim off to the left

So, weight over on the left side, left shoulder down and right shoulder up, hands well ahead of the ball, a steep backswing, and a big effort to stay down and go right through the ball on the through-swing. Why so many golfers miss this shot is because they don't stay with the shot and hit *down* into the ball. They feel, rightly, that it's going to be difficult to get height, so they try to put it on the ball artificially by scooping, which leads inevitably to fluffing the shot. You really do have to 'chase after' this one for good results.

Achieving height is always going to be difficult from a downhill lie, but you will get more distance than from a flat lie if you make a solid strike. Hence, be intelligent about club selection, remembering that the more lofted the club you are using the easier this shot is to play. Also, because you are over on your left side throughout, it is very easy to slice from a downhill lie, especially with the straight-faced clubs (which you would only try to use, of course, if the lie was *slightly* downhill). Always allow for this in your aim.

Ball above feet

How effectively you can play the side-hill lies will depend largely on your understanding of the basic dimensions of the game, for here swing-plane becomes of major significance.

The effect of the ball being above your feet is to make you stand more erect and farther away from it at address, and inevitably this is going to flatten the plane of your swing – it will

Opposite: An uphill lie necessitates tilting everything at address, i.e. so that the body is at right angles to the slope. The club can now follow the slope going back and coming through. You'll get more height than usual and tend to hook this one, so make the appropriate allowances

be more rotary and less up and down than from a level lie. The effect of this, in turn, will be to send your backswing and through-swing more 'inside' the target-line, and also to produce a more shut-clubfaced attack on the ball. In other words, whatever club you are using, your action will be of a distinctly sweeping nature, and you will certainly tend to hook the shot to some degree.

The way to tackle it, therefore, is to swing as the situation demands and allow for the ball's 'bend' by aiming off to the right at address. If the ball is only slightly above your feet, make a small adjustment of aim at address; increase the allowance relative to the height of the ball above your feet and the resulting flatness of your swing.

This is one of those shots where a clear mind's-eye picture of how you will swing and how the ball will behave becomes essential. Don't try to be too clever. Devote your energy to working out the degree of hook that will naturally result from your set-up and swing-plane, then play the shot as naturally as possible allowing for that flight. A little practice will quickly teach you what to expect.

Ball below feet

Playing a ball that is lying below your feet will similarly test your understand-

A downhill lie again necessitates setting-up so that you can swing downhill along the slope, as seen here. Again, the body is set at right angles to the slope. This shot will fly lower than normal so plan accordingly. It is a tough shot, so make sure you have plenty of loft on the club

ing of swing-plane.

In this case, simply to reach down sufficiently to make contact, you are going to have to lean over quite a lot and stand close to the ball at address. This will result in a steep swing-plane – a sharp up-and-down rather than a sweeping, rotary clubhead path – and an open-clubfaced attack on the ball. You will be able to make little body pivot and will be hitting very steeply into the ball chiefly with your hands and arms. The outcome will almost certainly be a degree of slice-spin.

The way to tackle this shot, as with the previous one, is to swing as the slope demands, and simply allow for the ball's left-to-right trajectory by aiming off to the left at address. Again, try to 'picture' the shot in your mind's-eye. If the ball is only a little way below your feet, aim the shot only fractionally left at address. The lower the ball gets, and the nearer to it you must stand, the more you must aim off to allow for the bigger slice that will result.

Even quite competent golfers sometimes come unstuck over some of the sloping lies that occur commonly in golf, but I am sure they wouldn't if they simply took the trouble to think out each shot before applying the club. Because, once you know the game's basic mechanics, really all any of these situations require are a common-sense approach and a swing that naturally fits the circumstances, instead of fighting them.

11
Bunker Play
Taking the terror out of sand

Most club golfers will have heard the claim of professionals that bunker shots are the easiest in golf. Few will have agreed, and there are three good reasons for their scepticism. The first is that many club players don't have the right club for getting out of sand; the second is that they don't know the correct methods; and the third is that they are frightened of bunkers because they have never practised from them.

To play effective sand shots you must, first, have a proper sand club, a broad-soled wedge in which the flange extends below the leading edge of the blade. The design of this club allows it to slide easily through the sand and under the ball without digging and deceleration. As the old masters proved, good bunker shots are possible with ordinary pitching clubs, but they are much more difficult than with the modern, purpose-built sand-wedge.

Having got the right club, you must develop and *practise* the right methods. The method of playing a straightforward greenside bunker shot is basically very simple, and once you know it,

your fear of leaving the ball in the sand should be gone for ever. But to get the ball repeatedly close to the hole, as the pro's do, requires more than method: it requires experience of varying sand situations and conditions, and you'll only get that from practice.

The prime objective in playing a greenside bunker shot from a normal lie is to slide the clubface through the sand *under* the ball. To enable it to do that the clubface should be slightly *open* as it moves into and through the sand. Any tendency to close it will cause the sharp leading edge to dig into the sand, slowing down or stopping the club with fatal results (and it is, in fact, because they swing in a way that closes the clubface that so many handicap players are such dismal performers from sand).

As always, the set-up is vital. Start by addressing the ball with the club-face open – the more open the less distance and greater height you need – and play the ball well forward, opposite your left heel. Keep your hands level with the ball, not 'leading' it. This

76

The standard greenside bunker shot. Ball forward; clubface and
shoulders open; slow, easy, full swing following the shoulder line;
complete hip clearance on the through-swing to keep the clubface
open as it slides through the sand beneath the ball. Be sure to
follow-through

alignment will tend to pull your shoulders into an open position. Ensure that they *are* so aligned. Have the feeling that the clubface is aimed to the right of the target and that your shoulders are aimed a corresponding amount to the left. For a fairly long, strong shot, the amount both your clubface and shoulder are aimed off in opposing directions would be just a few degrees. For a very short, high, 'soft' shot, the clubface would be pointing well right of target, and your shoulders well left – up to 45 degrees in either direction for a little 'pop' shot.

Your natural line of swing from this set-up will be out-to-in, and this in itself encourages an open-clubface attack on the ball, and also steepens the swing so that the club will slide *under* the ball. So, take the club back smoothly, slowly, and *fully* with your arms and hands, swinging naturally on the out-to-in line you have established. Let your wrists cock naturally. Do not consciously pivot your shoulders, but stay relaxed and 'easy' in your upper body and flexible in your knees.

And here we come to the vital move, where so many club players fall down. Still maintaining a slow, fluid rhythm, *get your hips moving and keep them going* as you slide the clubhead into the sand and under the ball in the through-swing. Whatever else happens, keep those hips turning and opening as you apply the clubhead, because this is the only way you can move the club through the ball with the face open. If you throw the club to the ball with your

hands and arms without your hips clearing, the clubface will be closed and will decelerate at impact or bury deep in the sand and stop completely. This is one of the commonest faults of the week-end golfer.

Remember that the object of most greenside bunker shots is not to 'blast' the ball out, but to float it fairly gently from the trap on a cushion of sand, by skimming the club easily just beneath the ball. I promise you that a little practice, an open set-up, a slow full swing, and an open clubface will take all the terrors from bunker play.

In other sand situations, other techniques are necessary. If your ball is plugged, or lying very much down in the sand, it usually becomes necessary to force it out of the bunker by hitting sharply and deeply down into the sand behind. In this case you must hood the clubface and lead with your hands both at address and during the swing, so that the sharp edge rather than the bottom flange is the first part of the club to contact the sand. Play the ball well back at address, stand square to the target, pick the club up steeply, and swing it sharply down into the sand an inch or two behind the ball. Don't worry about following-through – concentrate on getting the club right down and under the ball. Allow for a

Opposite: A plugged ball should be addressed opposite the right foot with the clubface hooded *(bottom right)*. The backswing is steep, making it possible to hit strongly *down* two or three inches behind the ball. The follow-through is restricted and the ball will tend to roll

79

lot of run – you can apply very little backswing with this type of shot. Also, if you have a steep bank ahead, consider whether you can achieve enough height to get the ball out forwards. You might save a stroke – or a number of strokes – by playing out sideways, or even backwards.

Gaining distance out of sand, depending on the circumstances of the shot, is not as difficult as many club golfers think. The criteria are the height of the forward bank of the bunker and your lie in the sand. If the latter is good, your potential distance is regulated only by what club will absolutely definitely clear the forward bank (and my advice is to assess the minimum loft you need, then take one more club).

The technique here is much the same as you would use for a low, 'driven' shot from the fairway. You have to hit the ball 'clean' – if you touch a few grains of sand before you contact the ball, the shot will always die on you.

So move the ball back towards your right foot, stand square with your hands leading (remember this delofts the club, so be sure you've made the right choice), set your feet solidly in the sand, move your weight well over on to your left side, and make a strong arm-swing with not too much body movement – keep the swing short and firm as you would for a 'punch' shot under the wind. Coming down, be sure to lead with your hips and to keep them going, so that your hands lead the clubhead into the ball before your wrists uncock. Try to hit *down* the back of the ball, taking your divot well ahead of where the ball lay.

Given the right circumstances, you can play this sort of shot with any club from a four-wood down, but the vital factor is always the height of the bank ahead. If you have any doubts, sacrifice a little distance in order to be absolutely sure that you will be hitting your next shot from grass.

So much for the basic bunker-shot techniques. None of them are especially difficult, but, if only because the composition and condition of bunkers vary so greatly, they do require experience. And that, I'm afraid, is just another word for practice.

12
Faults
Causes and cures reviewed

Ask a hundred golfers what are their faults, and ninety-nine will produce clichés of swing technique: 'Head up', 'I sway', 'My right elbow isn't in the right position', and so on, *ad infinitum*. The one who doesn't will usually be a good player, or potentially a good player. Through experience or study – or the help of a competent professional – he will have learned to put cause before effect. He will know that, *fundamentally*, a golfer can only commit three faults singly or in combination: that every bad shot he hits happens, *at root,* because at impact his clubface is open or closed, his line of swing is out-to-in or in-to-out, and his angle of clubhead approach is too steep or too shallow.

This one-in-a-hundred golfer will not need to consume millions of words of printed swing theory, take endless lessons from thirty different teachers, hit five hundred experimental shots a day.

I teach by watching the line of the swing and the flight of the ball, which tell me with certainty the position of the clubface at impact. This is vital to diagnosing swing faults

He will be able to tell from the *flight of the ball* what is going wrong at impact, and from that will know exactly what adjustments he must make to produce his best golf. In short, he will have the knowledge to reach his full physical potential at the game, with only time and opportunity to limit his ultimate development. In the hope that I can persuade a lot more at present frustrated people to tackle the game this way, I want in this penultimate chapter to ask them to look again at the things they do wrong in this dimensional context.

Slicing

This left-to-right shot, the commonest of all mishits, arises from a combination of three faults: the clubface is open to both the swing-line and target-line at impact; the swing-line is out-to-in across the target-line; and the angle of attack is too steep.

The cure starts in the grip, which must be strengthened until the ball no longer bends in the air but flies straight in the direction in which it was started, indicating that the clubface is square to the swing-line. To achieve this the hands must sometimes be placed more to the right on the club; in many cases simply squaring up the shoulders to the target-line at address will do the job, because it has the corollary effect of moving the hands from left to right in their relationship to the clubface.

Co-ordinating the swing-line with the target-line involves squaring-up the shoulders at address, so that they are parallel rather than open to the target-line, then making a 90 degree shoulder-turn while the hands and arms swing the club up and around, pointing the club at the target in the correct plane. Coming back to the ball, the hands and arms must swing the club at the same time as the hips open towards the target. Remember that if the hips and shoulders get too far ahead of the arms, the club will be thrown out across the target-line, even from a good backswing.

Flattening the angle of attack necessitates setting-up and maintaining a shallower swing-plane, by standing more erect at address from the hips to the shoulders, then *turning* rather than tilting the shoulders in both the backswing and downswing.

Bear in mind that these corrections interact upon one another. If, having previously aimed left, you square up your shoulders to the target-line you will automatically strengthen your grip and flatten your swing-plane.

Pulling

The shot starting and continuing to fly left of target comes from exactly the same set-up and swing as the slice, except that the clubface at impact is square to the swing-line (but is facing *left* of the target-line). The cure, therefore, is exactly the same as the slice cure, except that the grip does not have to be altered.

Topping and 'thinning'

Topping or 'thinning' – hitting the upper section of the ball – is a fault that accompanies slicing (particularly when the shots are topped to the left), primarily because of the steepness of the swing. The cure is the same as for slicing, with particular emphasis on flattening the swing-plane by standing erect from the knees at address, and turning rather than tilting the shoulders in the backswing.

The way you aim your shoulders influences your grip. The shoulder set-up here would create a hook, and it can be seen how this 'strengthens' the grip

Open shoulders at address lead to a weak grip and a slice

Heeled shots

Contacting the ball in the heel of the club again goes with a slicing set-up and swing. Because the clubface is open and coming across the target-line from out-to-in, the heel of the club leads at impact. Obviously, if you stop slicing, you stop heeling, and vice versa. Concentrate on swinging the club *down*.

Hooking

The right-to-left shot stems from the opposite combination of errors to the slice; the clubface is closed at impact; the swing-line is in-to-out across the target-line; and the angle of attack is too shallow.

The cure again starts in the grip, which must be weakened until the ball no longer bends in the air, indicating that the clubface is returning square to the swing-line. To achieve this it may be necessary to place the hands more to the left side of the shaft, but in many cases the grip will be automatically pulled into a weaker position when the shoulders at address are squared up to the target-line and the ball is moved correspondingly forward.

As with the slice, co-ordinating the swing-line with the target-line involves squaring up the shoulders at address, so that they become parallel rather than closed to the target-line. The club must point at the target at the top of the backswing, but in this case the player has to be sure that his legs and hips lead the downswing, and that he keeps them going to make room for his hands and arms to swing the club through the ball. Any holding back of the hips will slow down the arms, forcing an inside-to-out attack and a wrist-roll at impact.

Squaring up the shoulders to the target-line will automatically weaken a hooker's grip and steepen his swing-plane. From this position the main effort should be to swing the club *up* on target in the back-swing, and clear the left side in the through-swing.

Pushing

A shot starting and continuing to fly right of target comes from the same set-up and swing as a hook, except that the clubface at impact is square to the swing-line (but is facing *right* of the target-line). Hence, the cure is identical to that for the hook, except that there is no grip modification.

'Fluffing'

'Fluffing' – hitting the ground behind the ball – accompanies hooking, because of the shallowness of the bottom of the swing. The cure is the same as for hooking and pushing, with particular emphasis on steepening the swing-plane through the address set-up and backswing movement, and also keeping the hips unwinding, which will move the bottom of the swing forward.

Toed shots

Hitting the ball off the toe of the club goes with hooking. The clubface is closed and arrives at the ball from well inside the target-line, which leads the toe of the club into the ball first. Stop hooking and you stop hitting off the toe.

Opposite: If you wish to hit the ball straight it is vital that you start with your shoulders in the right position – parallel to the target-line as here

86

Shanking

Shanking – hitting the ball off the hosel instead of the blade of an iron – comes from involuntarily looping the club from inside to outside the target-line. Its most common cause is standing open with the shoulders, then trying to swing the club back on an 'inside' plane. Invariably this leads to a flat swing, and a flat swing leads to a reflex outward movement of the right shoulder at the start of the downswing, causing the club to be thrown forward so that the ball is hit off the hosel.

From the correct set-up, the shoulders pivot and with good hand and arm action the club will be in the correct position in terms of both direction and plane

The simple cure for shanking is to set yourself up square to the line of your aim, and then promote a feeling of swinging 'up and under' with the hands and arms, rather than 'around' with a big body movement and a wrist-roll on the backswing.

Always remember that the more 'up and down' your swing, the more difficult it is to shank, and the more 'around yourself' you swing the more likely this sickening shot becomes.

13

Four Final Thoughts

To help you play your best

The more I teach, play and watch golf, the more convinced I become that the decisive factor in good shot-making is preparation: shot assessment, club selection, grip, aim, stance, posture. If you can master these departments you have every chance of playing golf to the best of your full capabilities, whatever those may be. These are the spade-work areas; the foundations upon which your game must be built if you have the ambition and the opportunity to reach your full potential as a golfer. Of that I am totally convinced, and I am sure I would be supported in this view by the majority of the world's top players.

But there are a few other aspects of the game that I want to mention before we close, which golfers of all calibres tend to overlook or forget.

First of all, I would like to ask you always to remember with what you hit a golf ball. It is not your shoulder pivot, your straight left arm, your bent right arm, your knees, your hips, nor even your hands. It is *the head of the golf club*. In the last analysis, what golf is

all about is applying the *head of the club* to the ball as fast and flush as possible.

Now, this might sound rather an elementary point to labour, but I feel that it is increasingly overlooked these days, especially by beginners. We live in an age of applied science, to which golf has become subject perhaps more than any other sport. It is such a difficult game to play very well, and so many millions of people now want to do so, that 'method' has become almost a religion. Even though I teach individuals, rather than 'a method', I wouldn't argue with that. It is fun, if you are keen on something, to immerse yourself in the theory of it; and, so long as you are discerning and selective, it is often possible to pick up something of value. But do not ever let theoretical 'method' blind you to the basic objective of the game, which is to propel the ball forward with the *club*, not with some part or the whole of your anatomy. In short, whatever simple or complicated manoeuvres the search for better shots leads you into, don't ever forget to include among them swinging the clubhead into the ball.

This is especially true if you are a slicer, which 80 per cent of golfers are naturally. In the simplest terms, you never get the clubhead to the ball before you are past it with your body – you never hit 'early enough' *with the club*. If you want the fastest cure I know, simply hit shots with your feet together – and I mean *together*. That way you can only do the job with the clubhead. If you don't you will fall over.

The second thought I would like to leave you with concerns your own physical limitations. It is not easy to assess realistically and then candidly accept one's inadequacies, but doing so is a particularly essential operation for the golfer, because the game he plays is not one of power, but *power under control*. Nine out of ten pupils who come to me want to hit the ball farther. Very often I can help them, by showing them how to hit it accurately and solidly with an easy swing, instead of approximately and glancingly with a difficult or furious one. But what I cannot do – nor any other teacher – is increase their natural clubhead speed. Everyone has a definite point, depending on natural muscularity, co-ordination and playing experience, where he can equate speed (or power) with control. He should find it then play always within it if the score is more important than the exercise. This is a lesson that every successful golfer learned early and has stuck to. You will never meet a top tournament pro who swings as hard as he could physically, other than in exceptional circumstances for an occasional recovery shot.

My third point concerns your attitude on the golf course. In this book we have dealt only with half the game – the striking or shot-making side of golf. In many respects it is the lesser half because, even if you have the ability to hit the most perfect shots in the world, you won't win matches and tournaments unless you can play them strategically and tactically. So, whatever your limitations or advantages as a shot-maker, never forget to apply yourself assiduously to the arts of scoring. Bear in mind that many, many victories have been won, in first-class and club golf, by inferior strikers who could get the ball from A to B, over superb stylists and stroke-makers who couldn't answer the strategical or temperamental problems set by the course and the competitive situation. Remember that golf is a game of how many, not how; that people may often be interested in *what* you scored, but rarely in *how*.

Finally, I would ask you to do what sounds quite a simple thing but is, in fact, very difficult: to try your utmost on every shot. Golf can be the most frustrating and infuriating, as well as the most satisfying and elating, of games; but if it has one cliché that cannot be denied it is that the game is never over until the last putt has been holed.

So, don't give up – ever. Think about

what you are trying to do, which is to make a good impact. Think about what will help you to make a good impact, which, to put it as simply as I can, is correct aim and stance followed by two turns, one to get your body out of the way while you aim the club, and one to get it out of the way while you swing the club through the ball. Think out the shots *before* you play them, then think of one key factor to help you to swing as you have planned.

There's never been a greater game for triers.